The First

A (

Therapeutics

Nicholas Louis Hoesl, R.Ph.

VANTAGE PRESS
New York

To the only species that laughs or needs to

FIRST EDITION

Published by Vantage Press, Inc.
516 West 34th Street, New York, New York 10001

Manufactured in the United States of America
ISBN: 0-533-12176-0

Library of Congress Catalog Card No.: 96-90792

0 9 8 7 6 5 4 3 2

Foreword

In recent years, there has been an increasing emphasis on the value of humor, especially as it pertains to health. Our five senses are incomplete without the sixth, a sense of humor. As a pharmacist, I learned this long ago by collecting and composing words, quotes, puns, limericks, jokes, and treasuring stories I received from many sources. Some of the most original were from my patients and medical colleagues. And many of these humorous prescriptions possessed an enormous shelf life.

In this dictionary, I have followed the format of one of my early English teachers who asked us to first define the word and then use it in a sentence for further clarification. Mark Twain once reminded us to look for the hidden meaning in humor. This accounts for the "sly" part, or hidden ingredient, in the title.

I have often marveled at the quality, quantity, and longevity of medical humor originating from those who never had the benefit of a medical background, such as Ambrose Bierce (1842–1914) and Ogden Nash (1902–1971). You will find them generously quoted in this book.

Definitions or comments by the author are labeled N.L.H.; and others whose authorship is known are acknowledged. Many works I found to be anonymous, such as this one:

Humor is not a condiment;
It's a main course.
It's not a trinket;
It's a gem.
It doesn't need justification;
It's essential.

AAAAA

- a club for drinking drivers.
- *Addendum:* If you drink, don't park.
  Accidents cause people.

ABDOMEN

- The temple of the god, Stomach, in whose worship, with sacrificial rights, all true men engage.

Ambrose Bierce

ABDOMINAL

I sat next to the Duchess at tea;
It was just as I feared it would be;
Her rumblings abdominal
Were truly phenomenal,
And everyone thought it was me.

Woodrow Wilson

ABDOMINAL PAIN

- When I began practice—I was relatively safe in assuming (that abdominal pain) was appendicitis or green apples. Today it is also highly probable that the patient is suffering from the fact that his wife of forty years wants to leave him for the Peace Corps or Richard Burton.

Dr. Gunnar Gundersen

ACE INHIBITOR

- a trump card for one of life's bad deals.

N.L.H.

ACNE VULGARIS

- a dirty dimple
- Remember when the teenage drug problem was finding what worked on acne.

Now first he had acne vulgaris
The kind that is rampant in Paris
It covered his skin
From forehead to shin
Now they ask where his hair is.

ADDICT

- a crave slave
- one who believes that where there's life, there's dope
- when asked why he ignored the money when robbing the pharmacy, the addict said, "If I wanted money, I would have robbed a bank."

ADDICTION

- a junkie with a gift of gab.

N.L.H.

ADOLESCENCE

- just one big walking pimple.

Carol Burnett

AEROSOLS

- inhalant drugs, which if you are full of and sneeze, can cure someone.

AGING

- growing old is like being increasingly penalized for a crime you haven't committed.

  Anthony Powell,
  Temporary Kings, 1973
- It's better to be over the hill than under it.
- Every man is a fool or a physician at forty.

  Thomas Fuller, M.D.

As you age remember this
Always follow your bliss
With wine, wood, books and friends.
Old wine is best to drink
Old wood is best to burn
Old authors best to read
And old friends to love
If you run out of the above.

AIDS

- Senior citizens are the biggest carriers. Here's proof: hearing aids, Band-Aids, Rolaids, walking aids, Medicaids, government aids.

ALCOHOLIC

- someone you don't like who drinks more than you do
- they always seem to have a fifth sense
- some get drunk on water as well as on land
- a wife didn't know her husband was an alcoholic until the night he came home sober.

ALCOHOLICS ANONYMOUS

- a place where you can get drunk without being noticed.

- the difference between an alcoholic and a drunkard is that drunkards don't go to meetings.

  Jackie Gleason

ALCOHOLISM

- where no booze is good news
- I hate to advocate drugs, alcohol, violence or insanity to anyone, but they've always worked for me.

  Hunter Thompson

ALLERGY

- A bitch of an itch.

  N.L.H.
- We've made great medical progress in the last generation. What used to be an itch is now an allergy.
- The real difference between an itch and an allergy is about sixty dollars.
- I base my fashion taste on what doesn't itch.

  Gilda Radner
- Take calculated risks. That is quite different than being rash.

  George Patton

There was a young belle of old Natchez
Whose garments were always in patchez.
When comment arose
On the state of her clothes,
She drawled, "When ah itchez, ah scratchez."

Ogden Nash

ALOPECIA

- Hawaiian hair chant.

  N.L.H.

ALZHEIMER'S

- Of all the things I've lost,
  I miss my mind the most.

N.L.H.

- At my age, I've seen it all,
  done it all, and heard it all.
  I just can't remember it all.

AMNESIA

- nature's way of saying "Forget it!"
- doctors have finally solved this problem. They simply make patients pay in advance.

ANALYSIS

- a proctologists' tool
- in the final analysis, everything will come out all right.

N.L.H.

ANATOMY

- something that everyone has, but it looks better on a girl.
- the body is but a pair of pincers set over a bellows and a stewpan and the whole fixed upon stilts.

Samuel Butler

- hindsight can be a severe source of embarrassment.

N.L.H.

- She was insulted when a fellow asked her if she was familiar with *Gray's Anatomy.*
- The genitals themselves have not undergone the development of the rest of the human form in the direction of beauty.

Sigmund Freud

- I have everything now I had twenty years ago—except now it's all lower.

Gypsy Rose Lee

The limerick packs laugh anatomical
Into space that is quite economical
But the good ones I've seen
So seldom are clean
And the clean ones so seldom are comical.

ANESTHESIA

- an aroma coma
- a dose of comatose.

N.L.H.

ANIMAL HUSBANDRY

- a wife's nightmare.

N.L.H.

ANTABUSE

- the distillation of red ants to produce formic acid.

ANTIBIOTICS

- what you give to the one who has everything
- Chiefly the mold of a man's fortune is in his own hands.

Francis Bacon

ANTIDOTE

- body language
- My uncle is often quite caustic, but my antidotes on me.

APHRODISIAC

- a concoction
- R_x for Romance:

  Take the womb of a hare, fry it in a rusted, bronze frying pan, throw in three pounds of rose oil, then make it smooth with good smelling myrrh! Add four drams of fat, one dram of crocodile dung, two drams juice of garlic germander and of bloody flux, four drams of honey. Drink and get ready for romantic evening.

  Metrodora (Ancient Greek Physician)

APOTHECARY

- The physicians' accomplice, undertakers' benefactor, and grave worms' provider.

  Ambrose Bierce
- An apothecary should never be out of spirits.

  Richard Brinsley
  Sheridan
- Dead flies cause the ointment of the apothecary to send forth a stinking savour: so doth a little folly him that is in reputation for wisdom and honor.

  Ecclesiastes, 10

APPENDIX

- an organ that is useless to man but of value to doctors
- the lower portion of a book which nobody yet has discovered of any use

AROMATHERAPY

- paying through the nose.

  N.L.H.

- "Give me an ounce of civet, good apothecary, to sweeten my imagination."

  William Shakespeare
  King Lear

ARTERIOSCLEROSIS

- a soft heart and head to match
  Ashes to ashes,
  Dust to dust;
  If the cancer don't get us
  The arteriosclerosis must.

  Richard Gordon

ARTHRITIS

- twinges in the hinges
- caused by pain in the joints, which people should stay out of

ARTIFICIAL HEART

- Would you please turn on the television. I'd like to see if I'm still alive and how I am doing.

  Murray Haydon
  (artificial heart
  recipient)

ARTIFICIAL INSEMINATION

- population without copulation
- when you're number two, you better try harder.

ASPHYXIATION

- fanny fetish
- where the end justifies the jeans.

ASPIRING

- headache-prone.

N.L.H.

ASTHMA

- a disease that has practically the same symptoms as passion except that with asthma, it lasts longer
- Asthma doesn't seem to bother me anymore, unless I'm around cigars or dogs. The thing that would bother me the most would be a dog smoking a cigar.

Steve Allen

ATONIC

- Research suggests that one or two a day is beneficial.

N.L.H.

- The first glass for myself, the second for my friends, the third for good humor, and the fourth for mine enemies.

Sir W. Temple

- A little madness in the Spring
Is wholesome, even for the King.

Emily Dickinson

ATROPHY

- a posthumous award.

N.L.H.

- Sedentary people have shriveled hearts, and most of us who do not exercise have an atrophied body.

Dr. Bruce B. Dan

AUTOIMMUNE DISEASE

- a nervous wreck.

N.L.H.

Beneath this slab
John Brown is stowed.
He watched the ads
And not the road.

Ogden Nash

AUTOINTOXICATION

- never drive under this condition
- When patients say they treat their body like it's a finely-tuned automobile, always check the spare tire.

AUTOPSY

- the end result of not wearing a seat belt.

N.L.H.

BACILLUS

- a microbe on the make.

Frank Scully

BACKACHE

- man's greatest labor-saving device.

Joe Ryan

- a strange click-clack in the back of your sacroiliac.

Harold Rome ("South America, Take it Away")

BACK PAIN

- just a tension headache on a slippery slope.

BACTERIA

- the back door of a cafeteria.
  Before I heard the doctors tell
  Of the dangers of a kiss,
  I had considered kissing you
  The nearest thing to bliss.
  But now I know biology
  And sit and sigh and moan,
  Six million mad bacteria,
  And I thought we were alone.

BALDNESS

- a condition that may require a drug, a rug, or a plug
- Opportunity has hair in front but is bald behind.

  Aesop
- Hippocrates noted that eunuchs never lost their hair. This remains one of the few potential cures for hair loss that never caught on.
- What he hath scanted men in hair, he hath given them in wit.

  William Shakespeare, *Comedy of Errors*
- A hair in the head is worth two in the brush.

  Oliver Herford
- One remedy for baldness is made of alum and persimmon juice. It doesn't grow hair, but it shrinks your head to fit what hair you have.

BANDAGE

- the age when swing was king
- Big Bands: the music is gone, but the malady lingers on.

  N.L.H.

BARIUM

- what doctors do if the treatment fails.

BEER BELLY

- little more than a backup fuel storage unit.

BEDPAN

- The ultimate indignity is to be given a bedpan by a stranger who calls you by your first name.

  Maggie Kuhn
- Bedpandemonium: when all hell breaks loose.

BELLA DONNA

- a sight for sore eyes
- In Italian, a beautiful lady
  In English, a deadly poison
  A striking example of the essential identity of the two tongues.

  Ambrose Bierce

BERIBERI

On land or sea
One need not be wary
A well-made Old Fashioned
prevents beriberi.
Forget your hurry scurry
Downing two will undo scurvy.
And as for rickets
Why defy them?
When you can simply
Liquefy 'em!

N.L.H.

BIRTH CONTROL

- a misconception
- multiplication tabled.

BRAIN

- an apparatus with which we think that we think.

  Ambrose Bierce
- If the right side of the brain controls the left side of the body, then only left-handed people are in their right minds.

BREAST IMPLANTS

- They are not only a potential health hazard, but they violate the truth-in-packaging laws.

  Mike Royko

  Busts and bosoms have I known
  Of various shapes and sizes,
  From grievous disappointments
  To jubilant surprises.

  Waldo Pierce

BRONCHODILATOR

- horse serum
- enables a race horse to take several thousand people for a ride at the same time.

BROUHAHA

- a happy drunk.

BULIMIA

- where the pain in gain lays mainly in the drain.

CAFFEINE

- If it weren't for caffeine, some people would have no personality at all.

CALCINATION

- a country that spells relief.

N.L.H.

CALLUS

- the agony of defeat.

CANCER

- a smoking cure.

My final word before I'm done,
Is cancer can be rather fun.
Thanks to the nurses and Nye Bevan
The NHS is quite like heaven.
Provided one confronts the turnover
With a sufficient sense of humour.
I know that cancer often kills,
But so do cars and sleeping pills;
And it can hurt till one sweats,
So can bad teeth and unpaid debts.

J.B.S. Haldane, *"Cancer's a Funny Thing" New Statesman*, 1964

CARSONOMA

- a disease of nostalgic insomniacs.

CASTROPHOBIA

- a disease that closes in on Cubans.

CATATONIC

- spiked catnip.

N.L.H.

CAUTERIZE

- blinkmanship
- although he was near-sighted, he cauterized.

CHIGGER

Here's to the chigger
The bug that's no bigger
Than the point of a pin.
But the bump that it raises
Itches like blazes,
And that's where the rub comes in.

- Remedy for Chiggers: Apply alcohol and sand. The alcohol puts the chiggers in a frenzy and they all end up throwing rocks at each other.

CHIROPODIST

- a person who, when given an inch, will take a foot.

CHIROPRACTOR

- a slipped-disc jockey
- one who loves to manipulate patients.

CIRCULATION

- a tight girdle can both harm a woman's circulation and increase her circulation.

CIGARETTE

- a device with a fire on one end and a butt on the other.

  N.L.H.

CLAUSTROPHOBIA

If Christmas is a source of fear
Replacing the usual merry cheer,
Look beyond the holly daze and see
A New Year free of Auld anxiety.

N.L.H.

- TANNENBALM: an old German remedy.

COCAINE

- God's way of saying, "You're making too much money."

  Robin Williams
- Crack Cocaine: rocks in the head.

  N.L.H.

COCKTAIL

- an elixir mixture
- In 1793, New Orleans pharmacist A.A. Peychaud concocted a tonic of cognac and bitters, which he mixed in a double-ended egg cup called a *coquetier*. His American customers corrupted the name to *cocktail.*
- Cocktail Party: where you meet people who drink so much you can't remember their names

COLD

- a physical ailment that is both positive and negative; sometimes the eyes have it and sometimes the nose.

  William Lyon Phelps

  I am at this moment
  Deaf in the ears,
  Hoarse in the throat,
  Red in the nose,
  Green in the gills,
  Damp in the eyes,
  Twitchy in the joints
  And fractious in temper
  From a most intolerable
  And oppressive cold.

  Charles Dickens

- Cold in the Node: a drip tease.

COLD REMEDY

- a drug that will make you feel better, but not enough to go back to work
- If you think you caught a cold, call in a good doctor. Call in three good doctors and play bridge.

  Robert Benchley

- Fill mouth with water
  Sit on hot stove and bring close to a boil
  Your cold is gone.
- Pardon me to appear so bold
  In asking how you treat a cold
  "Feed it," they say, "is good advice."
  Or, was it, conversely, versa vice?

  N.L.H.

COLONOSTOMY

- when your colon is reduced to a semicolon.

COLOSSAL

- the large intestine
- Proctologists have assets of colossal proportions.

  N.L.H.

COMEDY

- a remedy of errors on others
- Commode: bedpan humor.

CONCEIT

- I-strain
- a disease that makes everybody sick except those who have it.

CONDOM

- (From the College of Condom Sense)
  Using a condom you will learn—
  no deposit means no return.
- —Condoms aren't completely safe. A friend of mine was wearing one and got hit by a bus.

  Bob Rubin

CONDOM CONUNDRUM

- A tisket, a tasket
  a gasket or a casket.

  N.L.H.

CONDOMS FOR WOMEN

- a product of congenial engineering
- We do not need condoms for women. What we really need is chastity belts for men.

N.L.H.

CONDOMINIUM

- a prophylactic for midgets.

CONTRACEPTIVE

- an article to be worn on every conceivable occasion
- The division between the sexes isn't as serious as the multiplication.

CONVALESCENCE

- I enjoy it. It is the part that makes the illness worthwhile.

George Bernard Shaw

- Get Well Card: The message doesn't matter if it's for a hypochondriac.

CONVALESCENT

- patient who is still alive.

Leo Michel, M.D.

COSMETICS

- applied art
- what women use to keep men from reading between the lines
- Never use anything that stinks, stings, or stains.

Guide to Miss Piggy's Life

- BEAUTY is in the eye of the beerholder

- RAVING BEAUTY: The one who finishes last in a beauty contest.

COUGH

- convulsions of the lungs, vellicated by some sharp serosity.

  Samuel Johnson
- something that you yourself can't help, but everybody else does on purpose just to torment you.

  Ogden Nash

  A cure for your cough that's precise
  Is a gallon of prune juice—on ice.
  You should really be told
  That it won't cure your cold,
  But before you cough, you'll think twice.
- SMOKER'S COUGH: It's not the cough that carries you off But the coffin they carry you off in.

COUNTERIRRITANT

- a person who should be kept out of the pharmacy, whereas over-the-counter irritants should be thrown out.

  N.L.H.

CRABS

- Never treat them; because look at what they're doing to you.

  Butterflies have wings of gold
  Moths have wings of flame
  Toilet crabs have no wings at all,
  But they got there just the same.

CRACKED POT

- a psychoceramic
- I was starting to crack up, but the shrink left me broke.

CREMATE

- a drinking and smoking couple.

  N.L.H.
- Never make an ash of yourself.

CREMATION

- zombie flambée

CRUTCH

- Reality is a crutch for people who can't cope with drugs.

  Lily Tomlin

CRYOSURGERY

- a sad operation.

  N.L.H.
- It takes a big man to cry. But it takes a bigger man to laugh at that man.

CURATOR

- a director of managed health care.

  N.L.H.

CUTICLE

- a delightful itch.

DANDRUFF

- suffering seborrhea.

DEATH

- just nature's way of telling us to slow down.

  Dick Sharples
- I'm not afraid of dying. I just don't want to be around when it happens.

  Woody Allen
- Live fast, die young, and have a good-looking corpse.

  John Derek, *Knock on Any Door*
- Die, my dear doctor? That's the last thing I shall do.

  Lord Palmerston
- In the end, everything is a gag.

  Charlie Chaplin

He was a cautious man,
He never romped or even played,
He never smoked
He never drank,
Or even kissed a maid.
And when he up and passed away,
Insurance was denied,
For since he hadn't ever lived,
They claimed he never died.

DECEASED

- the future tense of diseased.

  Leonard Louis Levinson

DEMENTIA PRAECOX

- precocious little demon.

  Richard Armour

DENTIST

- one who always looks down in the mouth
- someone who can bore you to tears
- one who after a carefree weekend is glad to get back to the old grind
- a dentist rarely asks questions that call for a simple *yes* or *no* answer
- Electric toothbrush owners are advised to brush twice a day and see their electrician twice a year.
- If God meant us to eat sugar, he wouldn't have invented dentists.

  Ralph Nader
- When your jaw is swollen, it's hard to transcend dental medication.

DEPILATORY

- a detox center.

  N.L.H.

DERMATOLOGY

- Itchcraft
- doctors who make rash judgments
- the best specialty—the patient never dies and never gets well.

DIAGNOSE

- best treated by a plastic surgeon.

DIAGNOSIS

- To avoid delay, please have all of your symptoms ready.

  (Notice in doctor's waiting room)

- [The joy of medicine is] the challenge of making a solid diagnosis, the delight in besting (if only momentarily) an intern or resident, the satisfaction (if rare) of actually helping someone, the sheer cantankerousness of being able to tell the bureaucracy to "stuff it."

  Dr. Michael J. Halberstam

DIAPHRAGM

- a muscular partition separating disorders of the chest from disorders of the bowels
- a slipped disc used to treat asphyxiation.

  N.L.H.

DIARRHEA

- may be hereditary if it runs in your genes.

DIET

- comes from the verb, to die.

  Art Buchwald
- what you get putting off while you are putting on
- Haste makes waist, so always eat slowly.

  N.L.H.
- I told my doctor I get very tired when I go on a diet, so he gave me pep pills. Know what happened? I ate faster.

  Joe E. Lewis
- My wife is a light eater—as soon as it's light, she starts to eat.

  Henny Youngman
- Don't diet, live it.
- My doctor's on a golf diet. He lives on greens.

DIETING

- Snackrifice
- starving yourself to death so you can live a little longer
- The two biggest sellers in any bookstore are the cookbooks and the diet books. The one tells you how to prepare the food and the other how not to eat any of it.

  Andy Rooney
- Don't be a refrigeraider.
- Before long it will be the animals who do the dieting so that the ultimate consumer does not have to.

  Mimi Sheraton

DIETER'S PRAYER

Lord, grant me the strength that I may not fall
Into the clutches of cholesterol.
At polysaturates I'll never mutter
For the road to hell is paved with butter.
And cake is cursed and cream is awful
And Satan is hiding in every waffle.
Teach me the evils of hollandaise
Of pasta and gobs of mayonnaise
And crisp fried chicken from the South.
Lord, if you love me, shut my mouth.

Dr. Steven A. Pickert

DIGITALIS

- an early form of arithmetic for counting up to twenty.

DISABILITY

- You are not crippled at all unless your mind is in a splint.

  Frank Scully

DISEASES

- the tax on pleasures.

John Ray, 1695

The rabbit's dreary eyes grow dreamier
As he quietly gives you tularemia.
The parrot closes his hooked proboscis
And laughs while handing you psittacosis.
In every swamp or wooded area
Mosquito witches brew malaria.
We risk at every jolly picnic
Spotted fever from a tic nick,
People perish of bubonic.
To rats, it's better than a tonic.
The hog converted into pork
Puts trichinosis on your fork.
The dog today that guards your babies
Tomorrow turns and gives them rabies.
The baby, once all milk and spittle,
Grows to a Hitler, and boy, can he hittle!
That's our planet, and we're stuck with it.
I wish its inheritors the best of luck with it.

Ogden Nash, "A Bulletin Has Just Come In"

DISTRESS

- a disease incurred by exposure to the prosperity of a friend.

Ambrose Bierce

DOCTOR

- a guy who tells you if you don't cut out something, he'll cut something out of you

- Heal thyself?
  Does a doctor doctor a doctor according to the doctored doctor's doctrine or doctoring, or does the doctor doing the doctoring doctor the other doctor according to his own doctoring doctrine?
- BEST DOCTOR: The best doctors in the world are Doctor Diet, Doctor Quiet, and Doctor Merryman.

  Jonathan Swift,
  1667–1745
- The best doctor is one you run for and can't find.

  Denis Diderot, 1780

DOCTOR FEE

Physicians of the utmost fame,
Were called at once; but when they came
They answered, as they took their fees,
"There is no cure for this Disease!"

Hilaire Belloc

DOCTOR TYPES

- D.O.—Doctor only
  E.R.—Doc in a box
  Sports—Jock Doc
  D.O.A.—Late Doc

DRINKING

- A problem drinker is one who never buys.
- Work is the curse of the drinking classes.
- Always do sober what you said you'd do drunk. That will teach you to keep your mouth shut.

  Ernest Hemingway

  A Frenchman drinks his native wine
  A German drinks his beer,

An Englishman quaffs 'alf and 'alf
Because it brings good cheer.
The Scotchman drinks his whiskey straight
Because it brings on dizziness
But we Americans can't choose at all—
So we drink the whole damn business.

- One more drink and I'll be under the host.

  Dorothy Parker

- Candy is dandy
  But liquor
  Is quicker.

  Ogden Nash, "Reflections on Icebreaking" *Hard Lines,* 1931

If all be true as we do think
There are five reasons why we drink:
Good wine, a friend, or being dry,
Or but we should be, by and by—
Or any other reason why.

Henry Aldrich

- A congressman was once asked about his attitude toward whiskey. "If you mean the demon drink that poisons the mind, pollutes the body, desecrates family life and inflames sinners, then I am against it. But if you mean the elixir of Christmas cheer, the shield against winter chill, the taxable potion that puts needed funds into public coffers to comfort crippled children, then I'm for it. This is my position and I will not compromise.

  Mark Edw. Lender and Kirby Martin

DRUG ABUSE

- Alcohol, pot, and tobacco do away with half of mankind, but without these, the other half would die.

- Water in moderation cannot hurt anybody.

Mark Twain

- There is more to life than increasing its speed.

Mahatma Gandhi

A lusty old lecher named Tim
Decided he needed more vim.
But he took the wrong pill,
Which made him quite ill,
And now he's no longer a him.

DRUG BUST

- an unexpected narc at the door.

DRUG LEGALIZATION

- a cop out.

N.L.H.

DRUG NAMES (of mistaken identity)

AXIDENT
ACOLYTE
ANTIDOPE

BELEAVE

CARDIZEM CD ROM
DAMNITAL
ENDABUSE
GISMO
GLO-LYTELY
HALFASPIRIN
INDERAM SUPPOSITORIES
MORBID
PROZAP
PHAZEME
LODINER
SINOMORE
TALWIND
THREEBLINDMYCIN
TUMORBID

DRUG TESTING

- urine trouble
- jar wars

  The boxing decree had a familiar sting.
  Drug tests for all who go in the ring.
  Those who defied heard the shout,
  "It's either urine, or you're out."

  N.L.H.

DUNLOP DISEASE

- an inflationary condition in which your belly has dunlopped over your belt
- If you're planning to retire, work on your spare now.

DYING

- Dying is easy. Comedy is hard.

  Edmund Kean, 1833, on deathbed
- We can now prove that large numbers of Americans are dying from sitting on their behinds.

  Dr. Bruce B. Dan

DYSPEPTIC

- a man who can eat his cake and have it too.

  Austin O'Malley

EFFERVESCENT

Here lies the body of Mary Jane Abbott
She burst while drinking an alka tablet
Called from this world to her heavenly rest
She should have waited till it effervesced.

EGOTISM

- the anesthetic that dulls the pain of stupidity.

Frank Leahy

ELECTROCARDIOGRAM

- ticker tape.

Lil O. Olson

- As for me, except for an occasional heart attack, I feel as young as I ever did.

Robert Benchley

EMETIC

- a substance that causes the stomach to take a sudden and enthusiastic interest in outside affairs.

Ambrose Bierce

EMOTION

- a prostrating disease caused by a determination of the heart to the head. It is sometimes accompanied by a copious discharge of hydrated chloride of sodium from the eyes.

Ambrose Bierce

ENDOSCOPE

- the last look.

N.L.H.

ENEMA

- not a friend
- as a patient, never be your own worst enema.

N.L.H.

ENTHUSIASM

- distemper of youth, curable by small doses of repentance in connection with outward applications of experience.

Ambrose Bierce

EPILEPSY

- the survival of the fit.

ERECTION

- the stiff of life, the staff of laugh, and often vice versa.

ESTROGEN

- a female condom
- a request in Spanish at a drug counter
- CONJUGATED ESTROGENS: those that like to horse around.

N.L.H.

ETHNOBOTANY

- back to our roots
  Jaborandi, papain, curare, and quinine,
  The forest's the best for your medicine chest.
  Aware of these goods, you still chop down the woods
  You'd best spare that tree, cause it might help spare
  thee.

Jim Duke, Ethnobotanist

EXERCISE

- I get my exercise acting as pallbearer to my friends who exercise.

Chauncey Depew

- Exercise is bunk. If you are healthy, you don't need it; if you are sick, you shouldn't take it.

  Henry Ford
- The only reason I would take up jogging is so that I could hear heavy breathing again.

  Erma Bombeck
- I like long walks, especially when they're taken by people who annoy me.

  Fred Allen
- My grandmother started walking five miles a day when she was sixty. She's ninety-five now, and we don't know where the hell she is.

  Ellen DeGeneres

"I never see a jogger smile,"
I'm told by a blimp the size of a barn
Who can't run a mile.
"But isn't running rather boring?"
I'm asked by a colleague
Whose greatest exercise is snoring.
"Oh, I've heard it's hard on the body,"
I'm reminded by the expert
As she quaffs her fifth toddy.
In mythology Achilles' weakness
Became his terrible curse.
Just as these heels cause my distress
And surely are no worse.

Stephen Owen

FAT

- adipose complex.

FATIGUE

- The best thing to take when you're run down is the license number of the car that hit you.
- Today my heart beat over 103,000 times
  My blood traveled 186,000 miles
  I breathed over 23,000 times
  I inhaled 438 cubic feet of air
  I spoke 4,800 words
  I moved 750 major muscles,
  I exercised 7,000,000 brain cells.
  No wonder I'm tired.

FAMILIARITY

- Familiarity breeds contempt and children.

  Mark Twain

FEVER

- Some doctors are grateful for small fevers.
- FERVOR: fever with a purpose
- FEVER REMEDY: Put a person with a high fever in bed with a person with the chills.
- Once Antigonis was told that his son, Demetrius, was ill, and went to see him. At the door he met some young beauty. Going in, he sat down by the bed and took his pulse. "The fever," said Demetrius, "has just left me."

  "Oh, yes," replied the father. "I met it going out the door."

  Plutarch A.D. 46–120

FIBIA

- a small lie.

FIT

- an accident in a tailor's shop.

Cynic's Encyclopedia

FLABBERGASTED

- the shock of how much weight people say you've accumulated.

N.L.H.

FLATULENCE

- a way to unwind.

FLEAS

- One of the best things for fleas is to find them a nice dog.

N.L.H.

So naturalists observe, a flea
Hath smaller fleas that on him prey;
And these have smaller still to bite 'em;
And so proceed ad infinitum.
Thus every poet, in his kind,
Is bit by him that comes behind.

Jonathan Swift

FLU

- an ill wind that makes everybody blow good.

Lisa Kirk

- Whiskey may not cure the flu, but it fails more agreeably than most things.
- If everyone else has a flu shot, you don't need one.

A bunch of germs were hitting it up
In a bronchial saloon.
Two bugs on the edge of the larynx

Were jazzing a hay-feverish tune.
While back of the teeth in a solo game
Sat danderous Dan Kerchoo
And watching his pulse was the queen of the waltz.
The lady that's known as Flu.

Cal Beacock

FORMALDEHYDE

- saving your ass with class
- all dressed up to go six feet under.

N.L.H.

GARGLE

- hoarse liniment.

Edward Nietupski

GASTRIC

- blaming others for your own flatulence.

N.L.H.

GENETIC

- a lower priced drug.

GERIATRICS

- when your narrow waist and broad mind begin to change places
- when your back goes out more than you do.

Herb Caen

- It's the period of life when you buy yourself a see-through nightgown and then remember you don't know anybody who can still see through one.

Betty Davis

- To get back my youth I would do anything in the world, except take exercise, get up early, or be respectable.

  Oscar Wilde
- The best way to look young is to hang around with older people.
- If I'd known I was going to live this long, I'd have taken better care of myself.

  Eubie Blake

King David and King Solomon
Led merry, merry, lives,
With many, many lady friends
And many, many wives;
But when old age crept over them—
With many, many qualms—
King Solomon wrote the Proverbs
And King David wrote the Psalms.

James Ball Naylor

GERM

- a little bug with influence
- There may be germs in kisses. But you can bet that it isn't the germs that make kissing dangerous.

GINGIVITIS

- Fred Astaire's dancing partner.

GI SERIES

- military medics: LOWER GI—privates
  UPPER GI—doctors and other top brass

GLUTTON

- a person who escapes the evils of moderation by committing indigestion.

Ambrose Bierce

The influence of affluence
Makes this a land where fester all
The gluttonous diseases that
Are festered by cholesterol.
These coronary carriers
Evade the pampered foreigner;
Prosperity, it seems to me,
Is just around the corner.

E. Y. "Yip" Harburg

GOLD THERAPY

- a flash in the pan
- This condition has caused an outbreak of pandemonium in some hospitals.

N.L.H.

GRIEF

- If grief is a medicine, laughter is its antidote.

N.L.H.

GYNECOLOGIST

- a doctor who puts in a hard day at the orifice
- A male gynecologist is like an auto mechanic who has never owned a car.

Carrie Snow

HAIR

- Interest in hair today has grown to the proportions of a

fetish. Think of the many loving ways in which advertisements refer to scalp hair—sating, glowing, shimmering, breathing, living. Living indeed! It is as dead as a rope.

Dr. William Montagna

- The latest hair preparation is a by-product from the rain forest called Shamanpoo—a sperm-based shampoo that gives the hair a silky texture, but the hard part is keeping it down.

HALITOSIS

- a breath that takes yours away.

HANGOVER

- the wrath of grapes
- something to occupy a head that wasn't used the night before.

Howard W. Newton

HAPPINESS

- A good cigar, a good meal, and a good woman—or a bad woman. It depends on how much happiness you can handle.

George Burns

HAY FEVER

- flower power
- When the soft air is sweet with the smell of lilacs, men often attribute it to love, when they should attribute it to some drugstore.

HEADACHE

- an aspirin deficiency.

HEALTH

- It's no longer a question of staying healthy. It's a question of finding a sickness you like.

  Jackie Mason

- Early to rise and early to bed
  Makes a man healthy, wealthy and dead.

  James Thurber

- Health nuts are going to feel stupid someday, lying in a hospital bed dying of nothing.

  Redd Foxx

HEALTH BOOKS

- Be careful about reading health books. You may die of a misprint.

  Mark Twain

HEALTH PREVENTION

Mary had a little cold, but wouldn't stay at home,
And everywhere that Mary went, the cold was sure to roam.
It wandered into Molly's eyes and filled them full of tears;
It jumped from there to Bobby's nose and thence to Jimmie's ears.
It painted Anna's throat bright red, and swelled poor Jennie's head;
Dora had a fever, and cough put Jack to bed.
The moral of this little tale is very quickly said—

Mary could have saved great pain with just one day
in bed!

HEART

- From whence cometh the blood of life, the love of compassion, and the collective wealth of the A.M.A.

Johnny Hart, *B.C. Wiley's Dictionary*

HEMORRHOIDS

- a shrink a day keeps the doctor away.

N.L.H.

- A PENSIVE PATIENT: "Mr. Pharmist, do you have any supprisatories for hemorrhoids?"

HEREDITARY DISEASES

- Always bill these to the parents.

HERNIA

There was a young man with a hernia
Who said to his doctor, "Gol dernia,
When improving my middle,
Be sure you don't fiddle
With matters that do not concernia."

Heywood Broun

HEROIN

- THE PSALM OF THE ADDICT
King Heroin is my shepherd, I shall always want. He maketh me to lie down in the gutters. He leadeth me beside the waters. He destroyeth my soul. He leadeth me in the paths of wickedness for the effort's sake. Yea, I shall

walk through the valley of poverty and will fear all evil. For thou, Heroin, art with me. Thy needle and capsule try to comfort me. Thou strippest the table of groceries in the presence of my family. Thou robbest my head of reason. My cup of sorrow runneth over. Surely heroin addiction shall stalk me all the days of my life; and I will dwell in the house of the Damned forever.

HERPES

- The difference between love and herpes is that herpes lasts forever.

HICCOUGHS

- messages from the departed.

HOMEOPATHY

- dilutions of grandeur.

N.L.H.

The homeopathic system, sir,
Just suits me to a tittle;
It proves of physic anyhow,
You cannot take too little.
If it be good in any case,
To take a dose so small
It surely must be better still
To take no dose at all.

HOMO SAPIENS

- the only animal with brains enough to find a cure for the diseases caused by his own folly.

HORMONE

- an unpleasant sound.

HOSPITAL

- a place where people who are run down, wind up.
- a place where a private room has nothing to do with privacy
- a parked taxi with the meter running

Groucho Marx

HOSPITAL GOWN

- The first thing you learn from a hospital stay is that you're not fully covered by the insurance or your gown.
- a cloakroom rated G in the front and X in the back
- That's how they tell
  If you're well,
  'Cause the sickos never give a care
  About their underware.

N.L.H.

HUMOR

- emotional chaos remembered in tranquility.

James Thurber

HYPOCHONDRIAC

- one who can't leave well enough alone
- DOUBLE DOSE: We are so fond of one another because our ailments are the same.

Jonathan Swift

The Hypochondriac
When he moans of chills and fever,

Stomach trouble, headache pain,
Is he truly a believer
In his hurt or does he feign?
Can some secret, keen dislike be
Something he considers hid?
Does he have a shaky psychic?
Does his ego mock his id?
In short, is he actually stricken?
Or—just chicken?

H. Louis Hermance

HYPOCHONDRIA CURES

- One doctor cured the guy of hypochondria by telling him his insurance didn't cover it
- The best cure for hypochondria is to forget about your body and get interested in someone else's.

Goodman Ace

HYPOCHONDRIANTIQUARIAN

- one who tries to buy a stained glass thermometer.

Newords

HYPODERMIC SYRINGE

- a sick shooter.

HYPOTHESIS

- an essay on vaccination.

HYSTERECTOMY

- American spay of wife.

ILLEGAL DRUG

- one administered to a sick bird
- Some sick birds are better treated by quack doctors.

ILLEGIBLE

- script tease
- the mark of a true physician
- a doctor who skipped kindergarten.

ILLITERATE

- one who reads medical books.

ILLUSIVE

- putting off seeing the doctor.

N.L.H.

IMPOTENT

- having can'ts in the pants.

IMPREGNATION

- an X-rated country.

INCOMPATIBILITY

- when a drug loses its income and patent ability.

  N.L.H.
- OF PEOPLE: I believe a little incompatability is the spice of life, particularly if he has income and she is pattable.

  Ogden Nash

INCONTINENT

- Non Voyage.

INDEFATIGABILITY

- diet-prone.

INDIGESTION

- charged by God with enforcing morality on the stomach.
  Victor Hugo
- a disease which the patient and his friends frequently mistake for the deep religious conviction and concern for the salvation of all mankind. As the simple Red Man of the western wild put it, with it must be confessed a certain force: "Plenty well, no pray; big bellyache, heap God."
  Ambrose Bierce

INDISPENSABLE

- a pharmacy consultant.
  N.L.H.

INDULGENT

'Twas an evening in November
And I very well remember
I was walking down the street in drunken pride.
But my knees were all aflutter
So I landed in the gutter,
And a pig came up and lay down by my side.
Yes, I lay there in the gutter,
Thinking thoughts I could not utter,
When a girl passing by did softly say,
"You can tell a man that boozes

By the company he chooses"—
At that the pig got up and walked away.

INFANTILE

- an alimentary canal with a loud voice at one end and no responsibility at the other.

INFATUATE

- is equal to IN-FAT-U-DIE
- Has it ever struck you that there's a thin person inside of every fat one, just as they say there's a statue inside every block of stone?

George Orwell

INFATUATION

- when men lean toward big women, but not enough to altar their stance.

N.L.H.

INFIDELITY

- I feel more confident and more satisfied when I reflect that I have two professions and not one. Medicine is my lawful wife and literature is my mistress. When I get tired of one, I spend the night with the other. Though it's disorderly it's not so dull and besides, neither really loses anything through my infidelity.

Anton Chekov, M.D.

INNUENDO

- not to be taken orally

- FROM ANGRY PATIENT: "For all the good they did me I could have shoved them up my you know what."

INSANITY

- It's hereditary—you can get it from your children.

  Sam Levenson
- We go by major vote, and if the majority are insane, the sane must go to the hospital.

  Horace Mann

INSOMNIA

- the triumph of mind over mattress
- a person who can't sleep because he worries about it and worries about it because he can't sleep.

  Franklin P. Adams

INTERCOURSE

- shop talk for the jet set.

INTERNIST

- a doctor who specializes in general practice.

IRRITABLE

- Women are more irritable than men, the reason being that men are more irritating.

JOCULAR

- sportsminded
- The mold out of which good skiers are cast is usually plaster of paris.

  Art Buchwald

- WATER SKIING: a rich man's enema. I tried it once, but couldn't get the boat up the hill.

KLEPTOMANIAC

- a person who takes things from you before you lose them
- a person who helps himself because he can't help himself.

Henry Morgan

LARYNGITIS

- Try listening for a change.
- Keep your chin up. It helps keep your mouth shut.

Lou Erickson

LAUGHTER

- clonic tonic
- a medicine lacking in side effects except for those who die from it.

N.L.H.

- Laffing is the sensation of feeling good all over and showing it principally in one spot.

Josh Billings

- It is a form of internal jogging. It moves your internal organs around. It enhances respiration. It is an igniter of great expectations.

Norman Cousins

- an interior convulsion producing a distortion of the features and accompanied by inarticulate noises. It is infectious and, though intermittent, incurable.

Ambrose Bierce

LAXITY

- poor bowel habits.

N.L.H.

- I have come to the conclusion that a good reliable set of bowels is worth more to man than any set of brains.

  Josh Billings
- The general practitioner's association with the bowels begins with the digestion of large amounts of information at medical school. Quite often the intellectual nutrition is in a high fiber form, much of it is unabsorbed and goes straight through.

  Cliff Hawkins, *Alimentary, My Dear*
  Oxford, England
- Life is like a box of chocolate laxatives. You never know what you're going to get.

  Forrest Gump

LAZINESS

- is nothing more than the habit of resting before you get tired.

  Jules Renard

LIBIDO

- the urge to merge
- The summer cologne was supposed to repel insects and attract men, but they are still trying to get the bugs out of it.

LICE

- Anyone who has lice ought to have their head examined.
- What's the difference between lice and crabs? One crawls while the other talks.

  N.L.H.

LIPOSUCTION

- a kissing disease

N.L.H.

- letting the fat out of the bag.

N.L.H.

LIQUIDATE

- cocktails for two or more.

N.L.H.

- BOURBON: a corny liquid, containing sugar and alcohol. The corn gives you courage, the sugar gives you energy, and the alcohol gives you ideas on what to do with all that courage and energy.

LISP

- to call a spade a thpade
- Thespian: a lesbian who lisps

LITMUS

- test for a drunken rodent who shall remain anonymous.

LOBOTOMY

- better a free bottle in front of me than a prefrontal lobotomy.

Dorothy Parker

LOCKJAW

- a halitosis remedy.

LONGEVITY

- He who laughs, lasts.

Mary Pettibone Poole

LOVE

- heartburn
- softening of the heartery
- a grave mental disease.

Plato

- Platonic love is from the neck up.

Thyra Samter Winslow

- Love is like measles, we all have to go through it.

Jerome K. Jerome

- a dirty trick played on us to achieve the continuation of the species.

W. Somerset Maugham

Oh, innocent victim of Cupid,
Remember this terse little verse:
To let a fool kiss you is stupid,
To let a kiss fool you is worse.

E. Y. "Yip" Harburg

MACULAR DEGENERATION

- fast food dilemma.

N.L.H.

MA-HUANG (EPHEDRA)

- wife of Peking Man.

N.L.H.

MAINLINING

- vein pursuit.

MALADY

- female disorder.

MALE MENOPAUSE

- the time when a man starts to turn off the lights for economical rather than romantic reasons.

John Merino

MALICE

- nits happen.

MALNUTRITION

Cholesterol is poisonous
So never, never eat it.
Sugar too, may murder you,
There is no way to beat it.
And fatty food may do you in,
Be certain to avoid it.
Some food is rich in vitamins
But processing destroys it.
So let your life be ordered
By each documented fact
And die of malnutrition
But with arteries intact.

MAMMOGRAM

- a gynecologist's "Hello."

N.L.H.

MARIJUANA

- a trance plant
- GLASS BLOWER'S DEMISE

  Once there was a man of class
  Who loved to blow glass and grass,
  Inhaling 'til he became insane
  His legacy remains a stomach pane.

  N.L.H.

MASSEUR

- a limberjack who leaves no stern untoned.

MATERNITY

- is a matter of fact—paternity is a matter of speculation.

  H. Gideon Wells

MATERNITY WARD

- a womb with a view.

MEDICAL ADVERTISING

- Businessmen ran out of parts of the body. We had headaches for a while, but we took care of them. The armpit had its moment of glory, and the toes, with their athletes' foot. We went through wrinkles. We went through diets. We conquered hemorrhoids. So the businessmen sat back and said, "What's left?" And some smart guy said, "The vagina. Today the vagina, tomorrow, the world."

  Della Femina

MEDICAL ART

- The art of medicine consists of amusing the patient while nature cures the disease.

MEDICAL BOOKS

- I went to a bookstore today. I asked the woman behind the counter where the self-help section was. She said, "If I told you, that would defeat the whole purpose."

  Brian Kiley

MEDICINE CABINET

- that great American tabernacle.

  Peter Fasolino

MEDICINE CHEST

- It doesn't take an oxymoron to know. It is well stacked or well stocked.

MEDICAL ECONOMICS

- "Don't you think, Doctor, you've rather overcharged for attending Jimmy when he had the measles?"

  "You must remember, Mrs. Brown, that includes four visits."

  "Yes, but you forgot. He infected the whole school."

MEDICAL GRAFFITI CHRONOLOGY

- —1940s—Spend one night with Venus and spend a lifetime with Mercury.
  1950s—Penicillin took the sin out of syphilis.
  1960s—Give me Librium or give me Meth.
  1970s—Discretion is the better part of Valium.

1980s—Real coke is the thing.
1990s—Give me Prozac or give me probate.

MEDICAL MALAISE

Laser-beam surgery
And test-tube babies,
Bypass techniques
And new shots for rabies.
Medical advances
Are dramatic and bold,
But here I sit
With my common cold.

Mimi Kay, *Wall Street Journal*

MEDICAL PROFESSION

- Because of public attitude, it is made up largely of trouble-shooters and repairmen, when maintenance men are what are needed most.

C.C. and S.M. Furas

MEDICAL SPECIALIZATION

- has reached such a state today that patients have to learn to diagnose themselves before they know which specialist to call.

Two Minutes With You

MEDICAL STUDENTS

- My students are dismayed when I say to them, "Half of what you are taught as medical students will in ten years have been shown to be wrong, and the trouble is, none of your teachers will know which half."

C. Sidney Burwell, *British Medical Journal*

MELANCHOLY

- the pleasure of being sad.

Victor Hugo

- He's simply got the instinct for being unhappy highly developed.

H.H. Munro

MELANOMA

- the part of the cantaloupe not to be eaten
- MALIGNANT MELANOMA: absolutely not.

N.L.H.

MENTAL HOSPITAL

- I was once thrown out of a mental hospital for depressing other patients.

METHYLPHENIDATE (RITALIN)

- Each morning we begin our school day with a minute of silent medication.

MICROBE

The microbe is so very small
You cannot make him out at all,
But many sanguine people hope
To see him through a microscope.
His jointed tongue that lies beneath
A hundred curious rows of teeth;
His seven tufted tails with lots
Of lovely pink and purple spots,
On each of which pattern stands
Composed of forty separate bands;

His eyes of tender green,
All these have never yet been seen.
But scientists, who ought to know,
Assure us that they must be so. . . .
Oh! Let us never, never doubt,
What nobody is sure about.

Hilaire Belloc, 1870–1953

MIDDLE AGE

- when you begin to exchange your emotions for symptoms.

Irvin S. Cobb

MINOCYCLINE

- low intensity exercise.

N.L.H.

MINOXIDIL (ROGAINE)

- keeps you from blowing your top.

N.L.H.

MIRACLE DRUG

- any medicine you can get the kids to take without screaming.

MISOGYNY

- women rubbed the wrong way.

MISTLETOE

- hollydaze
- a parasite for sore eyes
- IN SPACE: athlete's feet

MORTIFICATION

- I know a man who gave up smoking, drinking, sex, and rich food. He was healthy right up to the time he killed himself.

  Johnny Carson

MYELIN SHEATH

- a personal condom.

MYOCARDIAL INFARCT

- gas blockage.

  N.L.H.

MYOPIA

- hocus focus.

NARCISSISM

- love of drugs.

  N.L.H.
- PATRON SAINT OF ADDICTS: Joan of Narc.

NARCISSIST

- a painful pimple.

NARCOTIC

- a pain in the ear.

  N.L.H.

NAUSEA

- under the weather in the Bahamas.

  N.L.H.

NAUSEATE

- inedible.

  N.L.H.

- On a New York subway train, you get heavily fined if you spit. On the other hand, you're allowed to throw up for nothing.

  Lewis Grizzard

NAVAL SURGEONS

- proof positive that specialization has gone too far
- MERMAID SYNDROME: Navy psychiatrists have tried to analyze the problem of seminal vessels on the high seas.

NAVEL

- a dimple that wanted to become the center of attention.

  Ade Kahn

NECKING

- a lofty name for that low-down feeling.

  Sam Johnson

- Whoever named it necking was a poor judge of anatomy.

  Groucho Marx

NEEDLEPOINT

- the lost art of the addict.

NEUROLOGIST

- a twitch doctor.

Shelby Friedman

NEUROTIC

- a person who has discovered the secret of perpetual emotion
- a person in a clash by himself.

Al Bernstein

- a person who thinks the world owes him a loving.

Changing Times

- a person who worries about things that didn't happen in the past—instead of worrying about something that won't happen in the future, like normal people.

Reader's Digest

- A neurotic is a man who builds a castle in the air. A psychotic is a man who lives in it. And a psychiatrist is the man who collects the rents.

Robert Webb-Johnson

- We're all controlled neurotics.

Harry Reasoner

NIACIN

- We call it niacin, because who in their right mind would willingly swallow acid of nicotine.

N.L.H.

NICOTINE

- a compulsive pesticide
- NICOTINE PATCHES: One man hated them saying, "First, they were hard to light. Then they didn't last very

long." The doctor replied, "Try putting them over your mouth."

- NICOTINES: the dangerous years.

NOVOCAIN

- a drug that enables the dentist to get you out of the office before you know what's happened.

NOSTRUM

- aromatic grog.

N.L.H.

NITROGYLCERIN

- Pill Power
- Patient to pharmacist: "Are these the little pills I put under my tongue for vagina of the heart?"

NONSENSE

- the objections made against this therapeutic text.

NURSE

- To be a good nurse you have to be absolutely sterile.
- After two days in the hospital, I took a turn for the nurse.

W.C. Fields

- If th' Christian Scientists had some science an' th' doctors more Christianity, it wudden't make anny diff'rence which ye called in—if ye had a good nurse.

Finley Peter Dunne

- SIGN IN EMERGENCY WARD:
Interns think of God
Residents pray to God

Doctors believe they are God
Nurses are God.

- WAR(D) WORDS: "Would you like to speak to the doctor in charge or to the nurse who knows what's going on?"
- PRACTICAL NURSE: one who falls in love with a rich patient

NURSING

- a hospital hootenanny.

N.L.H.

NUTRITION

- Eat what you like and let the food fight it out inside.

Mark Twain

- The four basic food groups: fresh, frozen, fast, and junk.
- Old people shouldn't eat health foods. They need all the preservation they can get.

Robert Orben

OBESITY

- figure mortis
- surplus gone to waist
- the result of making you thick to your stomach
- a word to the wide is sufficient
- We tolerate shapes in human beings that would horrify us if we saw them in a horse.

W.R. Inge

- There's a divinity that shapes our ends,
  Rough-hew them how we will.

William Shakespeare,
Hamlet

ONCOLOGIST

- a doctor who never keeps you waiting.

N.L.H.

OPTHALMOSCOPE

- eye wash.

OPTIMIST

- an eye specialist
- In my next life I would like to be a pessimist. Then other people could spend all their time cheering me up.

Katherine Elizabeth Whitehorn

ORAL SUSPENSION

- lack of patient counseling.

N.L.H.

ORTHODONTIST

- someone who braces the kids but straps the parents
- one who invites you to put your money where your mouth is
- a lot of people have the reputation for being cheerful when they're really just proud of their teeth.

ORTHOPEDIST

- a marrow-minded doctor who always gets the breaks.

N.L.H.

OSTEOPATH

- one who works his fingers to your bones.

OUTPATIENT

- a person who fainted.

OVATION

- a birth response.

N.L.H.

PAIN

- an uncomfortable frame of mind that may have a physical basis in something that is being done to the body, or may be purely mental, caused by the good fortune of another.

Ambrose Bierce

There was a faith healer of zeal
Who said, "Although pain isn't real,
If I sit on a pin
And it punctures my skin,
I dislike what I fancy I feel."

The Week End Book

PAP TEST

- Never cram for this exam.

PARADOX

- the beginning of group medical practice.

PARALYZE

- a couple of untruths
- Pentothal antagonist.

N.L.H.

PARANOID

- I really wouldn't be so paranoid if everyone weren't out to get me.
- Whenever you see two psychiatrists, don't let that paranoia.

PARAPSYCHOLOGICAL PHENOMENA

- the perfect explanation to your spouse or children.

PARKINSONISM

- autointoxication
- the feeling you get when someone takes the last parking space.

N.L.H.

PATIENCE

- a minor form of despair, disguised as a virtue.

Ambrose Bierce

PEDIATRICIAN

- a small foot doctor.

PEDICURE

- temporary relief.

N.L.H.

PENICILLIN

- Prescriptions are preferable to surgery when the pen is mightier than the sword.

PENITIS

- writer's cramp.

N.L.H.

PERFUME

- chemical warfare
- body booze
- Much of it is made by the French
  Who say, "It makes considerable scents
  To spray it on negligees or negligents."

N.L.H.

PETTING

- the study of anatomy in braille.

PHARMACIST

- a pillar of society.

N.L.H.

- a licensed drug pusher.

N.L.H.

- R.Ph.: Regulated Pill Healer.

N.L.H.

- Elderly pharmacist: Not worth a dram when he loses all of his scruples.

N.L.H.

- Rural Pharmacist: one who is outstanding in his field.

N.L.H.

PHARMACOGNOCIST

- a crude pharmacist
- born-again plant worshiper.

PHILOSOPHY

- I've developed a new philosophy. I only dread one day at a time.

Charlie Brown,
(Charles M. Schultz)

PHLEBITIS

- often cured by a good dog collar.

N.L.H.

PHLEGM

- an early form of humor.

N.L.H.

THE PILL

- is tax deductible next year if it didn't work this year.
- Last night I had a dream that all the babies prevented by the pill showed up. They were mad.

Steven Wright

PILLAGE

- to plunder a pharmacy
- a pill for every ill
- Repeat after me. . . .
  This small white pill is what I munch
  At breakfast and right after lunch.
  I take the pill that's Kelly green
  Before each meal and between.
  These loganberry-colored pills
  I take for early morning chills.
  I take the pill with zebra stripes
  To cure my early evening gripes.

These orange-tinted ones, of course,
I take to cure my charley horse.
I take three blues at half-past eight
To slow my exhalation rate.
On alternate nights at 9:00 P.M.
I swallow pinkies, four of them.
The reds, which make my eyebrows strong,
I eat like popcorn all day long.
The speckled browns are what I keep
Beside my bed to help me sleep.
This long flat one is what I take
If I should die before I wake.

Dr. Seuss, Pill Drill *You're Only Old Once*

PIMPLE

- a dimple on the loose
- I had plenty of pimples as a kid. I fell asleep in the library. When I woke up, a blind man was reading my face.

Rodney Dangerfield

PLACEBO

- a hypochondriac's drug of choice
- It requires a great deal of faith for a man to be cured by his own placebos.

John McClenahan

PLASMA

- a blud lite.

N.L.H.

PLASTIC SURGERY

- when beauty is nip and tuck
- she gets her looks from her father. He's a plastic surgeon.
- She had so much plastic surgery that the crematory labeled her as non-biodegradable.
- When the woman had her face lifted and saw the surgeon's bill, her face fell down again.

PMS

- allows a woman, once a month, to act like men do every day.

P.O.

Before you utter this phrase
Beware of the meanings it may raise.
It's not of mail, nor prescriptions' brief,
But merely the habit of bodily relief.

N.L.H.

PODIATRY

- Great ache corns from little toe corns grow
- Time wounds all heels.

Jane Ace

- DANCING: Podiatry in motion.

POLLEN

I used to think that I could see
A pollen lovely as a tree
The sneezing wheezing of the masses
Caught betwixt the leaves and grasses
Unless the pollens start to fall

I won't find any rest at all.

N.L.H., "The Allergists' Lament"

POLYESTROUS

- horny animals.

POSTERITY

- where the end justifies the jeans.

POTASH

- a bhang over
- the only thing left the morning after.

N.L.H.

POTIONS (that stood the test of time)

. . . Filet of a fenny snake
In a cauldron boil and bake.
Eye of newt, and toe of frog;
Wool of bat, and tongue of dog;
Adders fork and blind-worms sting;
Lizards' legs and howlets' wing—

William Shakespeare, *Hamlet*

PRACTICING PHYSICIAN

- a hospital resident.

PREGNANCY

- Having a baby is like taking your lower lip and forcing it over your head.

Carol Burnett

- ADVICE TO EXPECTANT MOTHERS: You must remember that when you are pregnant, you are eating for two. But you must remember that the other one of you is about the size of a golf ball, so let's not go overboard with it. I mean, a lot of pregnant women eat as though the other person they're eating for is Orson Welles.

  Dave Barry
- TEEN PREGNANCY POSTER: Will your child learn to multiply before she learns to subtract?
- LABOR PAINS: previews of coming contractions.

PREMATURE

- a baby born before its parents are married.

  Leonard Louis Levinson

PRESCRIPTION

- hieroglyphics written by a physician and translated by a pharmacist into dollar signs
- P.S. on R_x: "I got mine. Now you get yours."

PROCTOLOGIST

- a doctor who can't remember faces
- one who always stands behind his work.

PROCTOSCOPE

- a rearview mirror
- a super dooper pooper snooper.

PROPHYLACTIC

- a milk-free diet.

  N.L.H.

PROSIT

- a Teutonic anti-depressant.

N.L.H.

In heaven I am told
"There is no beer."
All the more reason
We drink it here.

PROTEINS

- building blocks for all ages
- The only difference between men and boys
  Is the size of their toys.

PSYCHIATRIC EXAMINATION

- a checkup from the neck up.

Richard Wheeler

PSYCHIATRIST

- a doctor who doesn't have to worry as long as other people do
- a physician who hates the sight of blood
- Anybody who goes to a psychiatrist ought to have his head examined.

  Samuel Goldwyn
- the next man you start talking to after you start talking to yourself.

  Fred Allen
- After twelve years of therapy my psychiatrist said something that brought tears to my eyes. He said, *"No hablo Inglés."*

  Ronnie Shakes
- He is always called a nerve specialist because it sounds

better, but everyone knows he's sort of a janitor in a looney bin.

P.G. Wodehouse

- PSYCHIATRIST'S COUCH: where one lands after falling off his rocker
- CHILD PSYCHIATRIST: what a childhood I had. My parents sent me to a child psychiatrist. The kid was no help at all.

Rodney Dangerfield

PSYCHIATRY

- the care of the id by the odd.

PSYCHIC

- Why is it spelled with a 'P'?
  I don't know, but it pcertainly does pseem psilly.

PSYCHOANALYZED PATIENT

- altered ego.

PSYCHOLOGIST

- a head coach
- a man you pay to ask questions your wife asks you for nothing
- a bartender who hates to see a grown man dry.

N.L.H.

- FEMININE PSYCHOLOGY: being smart enough to ask your husband's advice but not being dumb enough to take it.
- CHILD PSYCHOLOGIST: one who never punishes his children because being a child of his is punishment enough.

PSYCHOPATH

- a laboratory physician analyzed.

N.L.H.

PSYCHOTIC

- You've no idea what a poor opinion I have of myself and how little I deserve it.

W.S. Gilbert

PUBERTY

- The cause of changing the voice at the years of puberty seemeth to be, for that when much of the moisture of the body, which did before irrigate the parts, is drawn down to spermatical vessels, it leaveth the body more hot than it was, whence cometh the dilation of the pipes.

Francis Bacon,
1561–1626

- PUB: where Bacon learned about puberty.

N.L.H.

QUADRUPLE BYPASS

- the ramp you missed four exits back.

Johnny Hart, *B.C. Wiley's Dictionary*

QUININE

- the bark that is better than its bite.

RABID FAN

- a drunk in a ball park.

Jimmy Cannon

RADIOLOGIST

- X-rated
- a doctor who sees right through you.

RECTALGIA

- a pain in the rear, mostly evident in others
- RECTIFY: If you could kick the person responsible for most of your troubles, you wouldn't be able to sit down for months.

REMEDY

- To do nothing is also a good remedy.

  Hippocrates
- (FOR BAGS): A cure for bags under the eyes is to sleep upside down. The bags often work through a less noticeable part of the body.

  Mary Dunn

  Doctor, hurry, won't you hurry up and stop my worry
  Can't you see that I'm all a-flurry
  I've been troubled with ailment greatly, here lately
  Headache fixer, oh, you wonderful prescription fixer
  Won't you tell me why my shoulders keep going in
  the air?

  Irving Berlin, *They've Got Me Doin' it Now,* 1913

RHEUMATISM

- nature's first primitive effort to establish a weather bureau.

RHINOVIRUS

- not an endangered species.

RHYTHM

- the birth of the blues
- What do they call people who use the rhythm method? Parents.

ROTAVIRUS

- the bug that's going around.

SCHIZOPHRENIA

- a state in which two can live as cheaply as one.

  Robert Williams
- I always wanted to be someone, but I should have been more specific.

  Lily Tomlin

SEASICKNESS

- crossing the ocean by rail.

  Hudson Newsletter

SEBORRHEA

- diarrhea of the scalp.

  N.L.H.

SEMEN

- Ecstaseeds
- the original controlled substance.

SEX

- God's joke on human beings.

  Betty Davis
- is a misdemeanor. The less you have, de meanor you get.

  Charles Pierce
- Some of us may recall the time when the air was clean but sex was dirty.
- The sexual revolution is over and the microbes won.

  P.J. O'Rourke, *Give War a Chance*

SHIN

- a device for finding furniture in the dark.

SHYNESS

- Scientists have found the gene for shyness. They would have found it years ago, but it was hiding behind a couple of other genes.

  Jonathan Katz

SEIZURE

- wrestling with yourself.

SILICONES

- funny-looking bras for those who love to make mountains out of molehills.

  N.L.H.

SINEWS

- bad press.

SITZ BATH

I test my bath before I sit,
And I'm always moved to wonderment
That what chills the finger not a bit
Is so frigid upon the fundament.

Ogden Nash

SKELETON

- bare essentials
- It was so hot we took off all our skin and sat around in our bones.
- SIGN OUTSIDE GRAVEYARD: Due to the shortage of manpower, graves will be dug by our skeleton staff.

SKIN

- is like wax paper that holds everything in without dripping.

Art Linkletter

Man is someone like a sausage,
Very smooth upon the skin;
But you can never tell exactly
How much hog there is within.

- I'm tired of all this nonsense about beauty being skin deep. That's enough! What do you want? An adorable pancreas?

Jean Kerr

- DRY SKIN: The poor guy lost all his body moisture in one sneeze.

SLEEP HABITS

- Early to bed and early to rise, and you'll meet very few of our best people.

George Ade

SLEEPING PILL

- what the hospital gives you after waking you up because it's on the chart.

SMOKING

- The only way to stop smoking is to just stop. No ifs, ands or butts.
- When I was young, I kissed my first woman and smoked my first cigarette on the same day. Believe me, never since have I wasted any more time on tobacco.

  Arturo Toscanini

SNEEZE

- much achoo about nothing
- I fear that one day I'll meet God, he'll sneeze, and I won't know what to say.

  Ronnie Shakes
- You must not sneeze. If you have a vehement cold, you must take no notice of it; if your nose-membranes feel a great irritation, you must hold your breath; if a sneeze still insists upon making its way, you must oppose it by keeping your teeth grinding together.

  Frances Burney, 1792

SNORING

- the sounds of silence
- sheet music
- Laugh and the world laughs with you; snore and you sleep alone.

  Anthony Burgess

SOCIALIZED MEDICINE

- free medical advice that is dished out at cocktail parties
- when the psychiatrist lies down on the couch with you

SOLVENT

- The trouble with chemists inventing the perfect solvent is that they have nothing to put it in.

SPECIALIST

- one who knows more and more about less and less.

  William J. Mayo, M.D.
- a doctor whose patients confine their ailments to office hours
- Today medicine is very specialized—I had a head cold and when it went to my chest, I had to change doctors.
- An internist is someone who knows everything and does nothing.

  A surgeon is someone who does everything and knows nothing.

  A psychiatrist is someone who knows nothing and does nothing.

  A pathologist is someone who knows everything and does everything too late.
- MULTIPLE SPECIALISTS;

  a rash of dermatologists
  a hive of allergists
  a scrub of interns
  a chest of phthisiologists
  a giggle of nurses
  a flood of urologists
  a pile of proctologists
  an eyeful of ophthalmologists

a whiff of anesthesiologists
a staff of bacteriologists
a cast of orthopedic rheumatologists
a gargle of laryngologists.

SPECIMEN

- an Italian astronaut.

SPINAL COLUMN

- add up the spinal column and get a disc count.

SPINAL TAPS

- the last song and dance.

N.L.H.

SPLEEN

A renowned psychiatrist described as mean
Was oft afflicted with low esteem.
Introverts Anonymous salvaged the dream
Of freedom in venting his spleen.

N.L.H.

SPRING FEVER

- when the iron in your blood turns to lead in your butt.

STETHOSCOPE

- a magnifying glass for looking into peoples' chests with the ears.

Leonard Lewis Levinson

STOMACH

- an organ that serves instead of a clock.

  Jonathan Swift

- He must have had a magnificent build before his stomach went in for a career of its own.

  Margaret Halsey

STOOL (SCATOLOGIC)

- It wasn't the canine who stoically stold in, stooled, and stold out again, but it was cat who cunningly crept in, crapped, and crept out again.

STREP THROAT

- hoarse and buggy.

STRESSED

- Think about it long enough and you realize it's desserts spelled backward.

  Dave Dorner

- But, Jesus, when you don't have any money, the problem is food. When you have enough money, it's sex. When you have both, it's health. You worry about getting ruptured or something. If everything is simply jake, then you're frightened to death.

  V.P. Donleavy

- How beautiful it is to do nothing and then to rest afterwards.

  Spanish Proverb

SUICIDE

- a permanent solution to a temporary problem.

  Phil Donahue

- There are many who dare not kill themselves for fear of what the neighbors will say.

  Cyril Connolly
- Dr. Kevorkian is being sued for malpractice. One of his patients lived.
- Razors pain you;
  Rivers are damp;
  Acids stain you;
  And drugs cause cramp.
  Guns aren't lawful;
  Nooses give;
  Gas smells awful;
  You might as well live.

  Dorothy Parker
- If you're considering suicide,
  It wouldn't kill you to call us first.
  281-CARE

  sign in Cincinnati Health Department

SUNBURN

- getting what you basked for
- a fry in the ointment
- I never expected to see the day when girls would get sunburned in the places they do today.

  Will Rogers

SURGEON

- a masked man
- a plumber who works standing up
- If a man still has his appendix, gall bladder, tonsils, thyroid, spleen and two kidneys, ten to one he's a surgeon.

SURGERY

- Before undergoing a surgical operation, arrange your temporal affairs. You may live.

  Ambrose Bierce
- Mirth's concussions rip the outward case,
  And plant the stitches in a tenderer place.

  Oliver Wendell Holmes, M.D.
- MINOR SURGERY: surgery performed on someone else.

TANNING BED

- frying on a layaway plan.

  N.L.H.

TEETH

- Always be true to them or they will be false to you.

TEETOTALER

- a gift of the spirit
- someone who practices moderation, to excess
- One reason why I don't drink is because I wish to know when I'm having a good time.

  Nancy Astor

TERMINALLY ILL

- the feeling you get when your flight has been canceled.

  N.L.H.

TETRACYCLINE

- a bicycle built for four.

TLC

- take lotsa cash.

TOAST

I've drunk to your health in company.
I've drunk to your health alone,
I've drunk to your health so many times,
I damn near ruined my own.

TOBACCO

Tobacco is a filthy weed,
That from the devil does proceed;
It drains your purse, it burns your clothes,
And makes a chimney of your nose.

Oliver Wendell Holmes, M.D.,
1809–1894

- Can one lose weight by smoking?
  "Give us twenty years and we will take all the weight off."

  The Tobacco Doctor

TOOTHPASTE

- an absolute waste of money if your teeth aren't loose.

TOOTHACHE

- a pain that drives you to extraction.

TRANQUILIZERS

- little pills that you take to keep from becoming a big one.

  N.L.H.
- The trouble with taking tranquilizers is that you find yourself being nice to people you dislike.

TRICHINOSIS

- a poke in a pig.

N.L.H.

TRIPLE BYPASS

- when a guy hits a three-bagger and forgets to step on second base.

Johnny Hart, *B.C. Wiley's Dictionary*

TUBERCULOSIS

- TB or not TB, That is congestion
  Consumption be done about it?
  Of corpse! Of corpse!
  For it's not the cough that carries you off
  It's the coffin they carry you off in.
- Dad always thought laughter was the best medicine, which I guess is why several of us died of tuberculosis.

Jack Handley

TYMPANIC

- drumble rumble.

ULCERS

- stewing in your own juices.

N.L.H.

- I don't have ulcers; I give them.

Harry Cohn

- The view that a peptic ulcer may be the hole in a man's stomach through which he crawls to escape from his wife has fairly wide acceptance.

J.A.D. Anderson

URANUS

- where those ought to go who don't know their asteroids from a hole in the universe.

N.L.H.

URINALYSIS

- is as good as ours.
- The patient intentionally poured some juice into his specimen bottle to confuse the nurse. She remarked that it looked cloudy. Before he downed it he said, "Let's run it through again!"

UROLOGY

As men draw near the common goal
Can anything be sadder
Than he who, master of his soul,
Is servant to his bladder?

- NOCTURNAL: Nocturnal enuresis is a terrible fate
  I try hard to make it, but always I'm late.
  My therapist advises, "Don't get so upset!"
  That's easy for him, I'm the one who gets wet.

E.C. Oliver Jr.

VACCINATION

- an ouch of prevention.

Joan Branson

- the medical sacrament corresponding to baptism.

Samuel Butler

VACCINE

- a microbe who saved its soul.

N.L.H.

VARICOSE VEINS

- congested vessels.

VAS DEFERENS

- A male pill could make a vas deferens between kids and no kids.

VD

- having a whoribletime
- nothing to clap about.

VEGETARIAN

- Veni, Vidi, Vegi: I came, I saw, I had a salad.
- Roots, fruits and nuts,
  Muscle, speed and guts,
  We're the guys who eat no ham,
  We eat no beef,
  We eat no lamb—
  We're vegetarians
  Raw, Raw, Raw!

  Bob Cummings
- Cannibals are not vegetarians. They are humanitarians.

VENTRICLE

- The doctor told the mechanic that he had a slow leak requiring a valve job.

  N.L.H.

VERTIGO

- where you would like to tell a lot of patients who don't have any.

  N.L.H.

- I didn't need my meclizine because I only had a short vertigo.

VETERINARIAN

- the best doctor because he can't ask his patients what is the matter—he's just got to know.
- If animals suddenly got the gift of laughter, they'd start by laughing themselves sick about man.

  Egan Friedel
- Dogs come when they're called.
  Cats take a message and get back to you.

  Mary Bly
- Cats are intended to teach us that not everything in nature has a function.

  Garrison Keillor
- OVERPUPULATION: a doggone catastrophe
- To err is human,
  To forgive, canine.

  Peter Mayle, *A Dog's Life*

VIRUS

- often used by doctors to mean "Your guess is as good as mine."
- VIRUS-X: started by people who couldn't spell pneumonia.

VITAMIN

- what a pharmacist does when a customer knocks
- The pharmacy was out of vitamin B12, so the patient swallowed a dozen of vitamin B1's.

WARFARIN (Coumadin)

- a D-concoction
- Beware of the doctor who tells you to take it with a piece of cheese.

WEED

- a plant whose virtues have not yet been discovered.

Ralph Waldo Emerson

WINE

- an infallible antidote to common sense and seriousness; an excuse for deeds otherwise unforgivable.

Elbert Hubbard

When you ask one friend to dine,
Give him your best wine,
When you ask two, the second best will do!

Henry Wadsworth Longfellow

WITCH HAZEL

- belladonna without the make-up.

N.L.H.

WONDER DRUG

- any prescription under two dollars.

X-RAY

- bellyvision
- a device which enables us to see how the bones in the back room are doing.

Don Quinn

- The elderly gentleman was so frail that the X-ray technicians simply held him up to the light.
- As the X-ray specialist walked down the aisle to say the marriage vows with a former patient, many wondered what she saw in him.

ZZZZZ

You say you need your Z's, you can't sleep?
You've exhausted your pills, you're tired of counting
    sheep?
Ever wonder what doctors do for sleep?
They dream of the Sleeping Beauty, their blessings,
    and little Bo Peep.

N.L.H.